The Official
CHELSEA FC
Annual 2012

Written by Rick Glanvill

Designed by Brian Thomson

A Grange Publication

© 2011. Published by Grange Communications Ltd., Edinburgh under licence from Chelsea FC Merchandising Limited. www.chelseafc.com. Printed in the EU.

Photography © Getty Images and Action Images.

ISBN: 978-1-908221-22-3

£7.99

Introduction

Everywhere you look at Chelsea these days there is youth coming through.

Right from the youngest ever Premier League manager, André Villas-Boas, to some of the most promising teenage players in the world – Danny Sturridge, Josh McEachran, Romelu Lukaku and Oriol Romeu to name but a few.

There are more young supporters going to games and wearing their Chelsea colours too. As always, we celebrate that future as well as the past here in the Official Chelsea Annual.

We are the Pride of London, so we will also take a look at the upcoming Olympics being hosted in our city.

There are goals, goalies, and an insiders' view of the brand new Chelsea museum.

In fact, you could say that as far as this season is concerned, we've got it cover-to-covered!

Hope you like it.

Contents

CHELSEA ALL-TIME HONOURS LIST

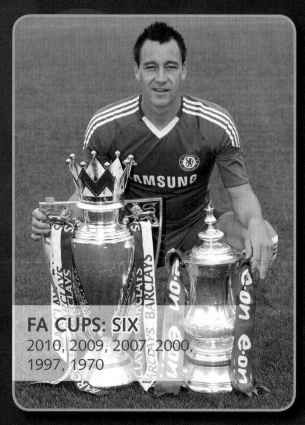

FA CUPS: SIX
2010, 2009, 2007 2000,
1997, 1970

**UEFA CUP WINNERS
CUPS: TWO**
1970/1, 1997/8

FA YOUTH CUPS: THREE
1959/60, 1960/1, 2009/10

LEAGUE TITLES: FOUR
2009/10, 2005/6, 2004/5, 1954/5

UEFA SUPER CUP: ONE
1998

LEAGUE CUPS: FOUR
2006/7, 2004/5, 1997/8, 1964/5

COMMUNITY SHIELDS: FOUR
2009, 2005, 2000, 1955

DOUBLE
WINNERS

09   10

THE NEW BOYS...

André Villas-Boas

He was one of the brightest management prospects around, wanted by a host of other big clubs. But Chelsea acted decisively and lured him away from Porto, where he had won the League, Uefa Europa Cup and two domestic cups.

André was at Stamford Bridge before, as part of José Mourinho's management team 2004-7 and is known for his attention to detail on performance, tactics and how the opposition plays.

Once in charge, he brought in two assistants: popular former Blues midfielder Roberto Di Matteo and Steve Holland, who won the national title as manager of Chelsea's Reserves last season.

Romelu Lukaku

Few players have made their love for a club so clear before joining it more than teenage powerhouse Romelu Lukaku. He visited the Bridge in a school trip in 2010 and was videoed saying that his one dream in life was to play on the hallowed turf. He also admits to sleeping in his Chelsea shirt. His hero is Didier Drogba.

Towering, muscular, very fast, he is already a full international at centre-forward for Belgium and has been a sensational goalscorer at every level for previous club Anderlecht.

❝ If I continue to improve my game I will change (the way I play) automatically, so I will continue what I am doing now and working hard. ❞

Romelu Lukaku

Raul Meireles

Midfielder Raul Meireles signed for Chelsea from Liverpool on a four-year contract in August 2011.

Born in Aves, Portugal, Meireles played for his national side, under Luiz Felipe Scolari in the lead-up to Euro 2008, where he scored his first international goal.

He spent just over a season at Liverpool with a low-key start, coming into his own in January 2011, scoring five times in six games.

Oriol Romeu

Barcelona did not want to let go of this extremely promising defensive midfielder.

Tall and powerful with good vision in his passing, he would have enjoyed many more starts for the Catalans had he not been injured most of last season.

He does the simple things very well and reads the game like a veteran. His presence in the centre of midfield is especially useful after Michael Essien was injured in preseason and will miss a lot of the current campaign.

Oriol is a player with a bright future. He is one of the most promising young players in that position 🙶

André Villas-Boas

Thibaut Courtois

One of the most sought-after young goalkeepers in world football, Thibault was snapped up from title-winners Genk in Belgium and immediately loaned to Atlético Madrid to further his development.

The teenager has similarities to Petr Cech, being very tall but fast and agile, and always in the right position to handle danger.

Juan Mata

Juan Mata signed a five-year contract with Chelsea in August 2011. He is mainly a left winger, but can also play as an attacking midfielder.

Since successfully graduating from Real Madrid's youth academy, he has spent the majority of his senior career with Valencia CF.

On his debut for Chelsea on 27 August 2011, Mata came on as a substitute and scored in stoppage time. Chelsea won the match against Norwich City 3–1.

Thanks and farewell...

Carlo Ancelotti left following Chelsea's 2010/11 season. The Italian will always be held in very high regard for becoming the first Chelsea manager to bring the league and FA Cup 'double' to Stamford Bridge. His assistant, former Blues star midfielder Ray Wilkins also ended his long association with the club, as did Paul Clement.

We also said goodbye to several players this summer, including Yury Zhirkov, Michael Mancienne, Jack Cork, and Fabio Borini.

Good luck to them all in their future careers.

🙶 Right from the first moment there have been good feelings all around me. Training has been great and the players are a great group to train with. 🙶

Juan Mata

2010/11 SEASON HIGHLIGHTS

Improving our most successful ever season was always going to be a tough task. While there were no trophies won, there were highlights to enjoy. Relive some of the highs and lows over the next few pages.

Fond Farewells
Summer 2010

In the close season we said goodbye to some truly great Chelsea players, namely Joe Cole, Juliano Belletti, Deco, Michael Ballack and Richard Carvalho.

Welcome to the Bridge, boys
August 2010

Our Brazilian contingent was topped up again by the arrival from Benfica, Portugal, of the man dubbed 'the blue Kenyan': Ramires. The energetic Brazilian midfielder's performances grew stronger and stronger as the season progressed. Israel international Yossi Benayoun also arrived, from Liverpool.

Chelsea 6
West Bromwich Albion 0
August 2010

Didier Drogba opened our Premier League title defence at the Bridge with a great hat-trick. Florent Malouda added a brace and Frank Lampard competed the scoring in our biggest-ever opening day win.

Wigan Athletic 0 Chelsea 6
August 2010

The Blues managed back-to-back 6-0 victories for the first time in our history at the DW Stadium. Florent Malouda hit an early opener, and Nicolas Anelka and Salomon Kalou two apiece, before Yossi Benaoyun scored his debut goal for Chelsea.

Didier rises in all-time scoring list
August 2010

His three goals put Didier ahead of the legendary Jimmy Greaves on Chelsea's list of all-time goalscorers. Jimmy scored 132.

West Ham United 1 Chelsea 3
September 2010

The Hammers became the first team to score against Chelsea, but by then two rare headers for Michael Essien and a Salomon Kalou goal had already sealed a brilliant win at the home of our London rivals.

MSK Žilina 1 Chelsea 4
September 2010

Daniel Sturridge made his first start of the season in the Champions League and impressed, scoring the fourth goal in a well-earned away win in Slovakia.

Chelsea 4 Blackpool 0
September 2010

When the Blues raced four goals up by half-time, everyone was expecting a repeat of the previous season's 8-0 win over Wigan – if not better. Instead, the scoreline remained the same, with Florent Malouda accounting for two of the goals.

Ossie statue unveiled
October 2010

1960s/70s icon Peter Osgood became the first Chelsea player to be honoured with a statue at Stamford Bridge. It was unveiled by his widow Lynn, watched by Frank Lampard and John Terry.

Chelsea 2 Arsenal 0
October 2010

Didier was Arsenal's destroyer yet again as he scored an unbelievable back-heeled goal. Alex almost stole the show with an unstoppable free kick. League leaders, happy days!

Spartak Moscow 0 Chelsea 2
October 2010

Yury Zhirkov volleyed one of the goals of the season in his hometown in this excellent Champions League win.

Chelsea 4 Spartak Moscow 1
November 2010

Progress into the Champions League knockout phase was almost guaranteed after this great win, in which Drogba scored his first goal for a month, and Branislav Ivanovic grabbed two to make it three in two games for the impressive defender.

Liverpool 2 Chelsea 0
November 2010

Future Blue Fernando Torres scored both for the Reds. A painful defeat.

Tottenham Hotspur 1 Chelsea 1
December 2010

Didier Drogba came storming off the bench to turn the game, hitting a piledriver past Heurelho Gomes to equalise the game. He had the chance to hit a morale-boosting winner from the spot. But with regular penalty-taker Frank Lampard having only just come on as a sub, the Ivorian saw his effort brilliantly saved.

Chelsea 1 Bolton Wanderers 0
December 2010

Our first win in seven league games. Florent Malouda scored too – his first goal for two months. Both sides had efforts cleared off the line. Not perfect, but we were back in the top four.

Wilkins departs
November 2010

Assistant manager Ray Wilkins left Chelsea, ending a 40-year association with Stamford Bridge.

United showdown snowed off
December 2010

A blizzard covered London and Chelsea's game against new leaders Man United was postponed along with other fixtures.

Chelsea 7 Ipswich Town 0
January 2011

Promising youngster Josh McEachran started in midfield and Danny Sturridge scored twice as Chelsea put the run of disappointing results behind us. Nico also hit two in an absolutely brilliant display against the 'Tractor Boys' in the FA Cup.

Chelsea 2 Blackburn Rovers 0
January 2011

The same scorers who beat Rovers on their home ground in October – Nicolas Anelka and Branislav Ivanovic – earned an important victory at the Bridge. It was the first time we had won back-to-back matches since that game.

Bolton Wanderers 0 Chelsea 4
January 2011

This was more like the old Chelsea. Didier Drogba thumped the opener from 30 yards, and Ramires opened his Chelsea account with a side-footer. Mikel returned from injury for the first time since December.

Fernando Torres joins the Blues!
January 2011

World Cup-winning striker Fernando Torres joined Chelsea from Liverpool minutes before the transfer window closed. He said: 'I know there are many great players here and I will work hard to win a place in the team. I hope I can score some important goals.' He was given a fantastic welcome by the Blues faithful.

David Luíz arrives at Stamford Bridge
January 2011

Brazil central defender David Luíz also arrived from Benfica and, with his outgoing attitude, clever skills and hair like 'Sideshow Bob' from The Simpsons, had an instant impact.

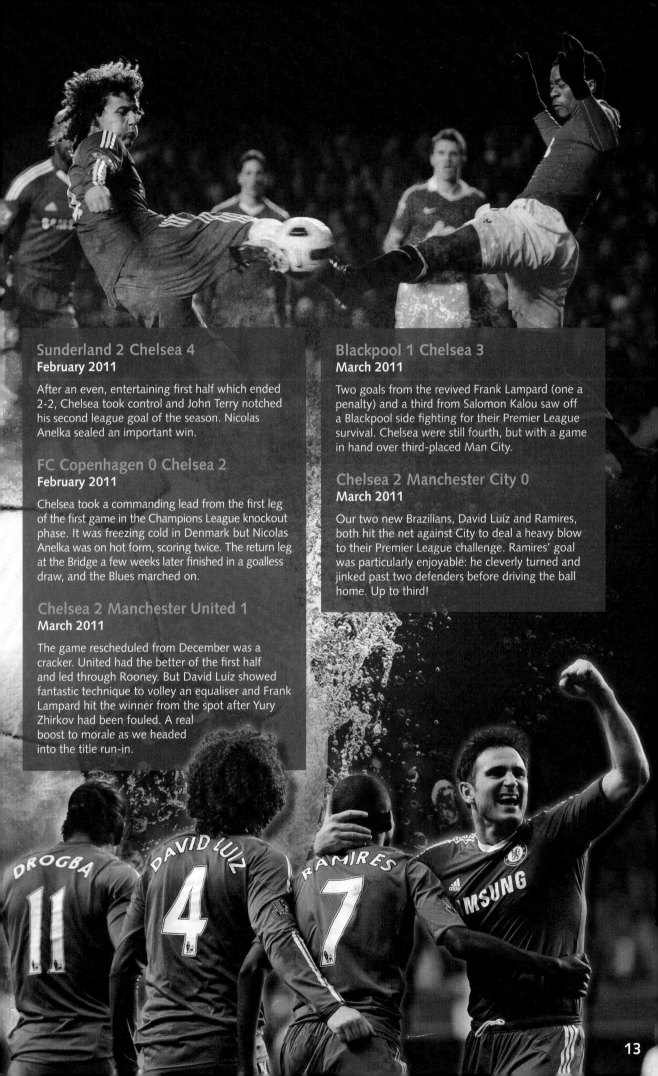

Sunderland 2 Chelsea 4
February 2011

After an even, entertaining first half which ended 2-2, Chelsea took control and John Terry notched his second league goal of the season. Nicolas Anelka sealed an important win.

FC Copenhagen 0 Chelsea 2
February 2011

Chelsea took a commanding lead from the first leg of the first game in the Champions League knockout phase. It was freezing cold in Denmark but Nicolas Anelka was on hot form, scoring twice. The return leg at the Bridge a few weeks later finished in a goalless draw, and the Blues marched on.

Chelsea 2 Manchester United 1
March 2011

The game rescheduled from December was a cracker. United had the better of the first half and led through Rooney. But David Luíz showed fantastic technique to volley an equaliser and Frank Lampard hit the winner from the spot after Yury Zhirkov had been fouled. A real boost to morale as we headed into the title run-in.

Blackpool 1 Chelsea 3
March 2011

Two goals from the revived Frank Lampard (one a penalty) and a third from Salomon Kalou saw off a Blackpool side fighting for their Premier League survival. Chelsea were still fourth, but with a game in hand over third-placed Man City.

Chelsea 2 Manchester City 0
March 2011

Our two new Brazilians, David Luíz and Ramires, both hit the net against City to deal a heavy blow to their Premier League challenge. Ramires' goal was particularly enjoyable: he cleverly turned and jinked past two defenders before driving the ball home. Up to third!

DROGBA 11

DAVID LUIZ 4

RAMIRES 7

SAMSUNG

Awards for David and Carlo...
April 2011

Carlo Ancelotti and David Luíz were named Manager and Player of the Month for March. It was Carlo's third such award, but David's was a quick reward for the impact he had made in two months.

Chelsea Academy 3
Manchester United Academy 2
April 2011

An FA Youth Cup semi-final for the defending champions, Chelsea's Academy, and a big crowd at the Bridge. The young Blues were missing the attacking influence of injured midfielder Billy Clifford, but raced into a two-goal lead before a more even second half saw United rally strongly. Unfortunately, it all went wrong in the second leg at Old Trafford, and Chelsea went out.

West Bromwich Albion 1 Chelsea 3
April 2011

The home side took the lead but Chelsea replied impressively. Didier Drogba, Salomon Kalou and Frank Lampard struck to turn the game on its head, and Chelsea were suddenly snapping at the heels of second-placed Arsenal.

Chelsea 3 Birmingham City 1
April 2011

The Blues dominated, with Florent Malouda netting twice and Salomon Kalou scoring a brilliant third. The Blues cruised into second place in the table on goal difference.

Chelsea 3 West Ham United 0
April 2011

Fernando Torres scored his first goal in a Chelsea shirt, prompting one of the wildest celebrations in years at a rain-drenched Stamford Bridge. Carlo Ancelotti's men were now just six points behind United with a trip to Old Trafford still to come…

Chelsea 2 Tottenham Hotspur 1
April 2011

The stadium erupted when Salomon Kalou pounced in the 88th minute to stab home what proved to be the winner. A day later Arsenal beat Man United and, incredibly, Chelsea were just three points off the top of the table.

Manchester United 2 Chelsea 1
May 2011

Chelsea had clawed back United's lead in the Premier League from fifteen points in March to just three going into this showdown. Unfortunately, the Blues gave themselves little chance by starting sluggishly. Frank Lampard pulled a goal back with 20 minutes remaining, but it was a disappointing performance.

Chelsea 2 Newcastle United 2
May 2011

The last home match of the season saw Chelsea lead twice and let the Geordies back into it each time. Alex and Branislav Ivanovic scored for the Blues. It was not the end to the season Carlo Ancelotti would have chosen, and it was the last time supporters would see him at Stamford Bridge as manager.

Chelsea Reserves 1
Blackburn Rovers Reserves 1
May 2011

Chelsea won the national play-off for the Reserves league title by beating Blackburn 5-4 on penalties. It is the first trophy the Chelsea Reserves have won since 1992, and suggests that the future is bright.

CHELSEA SQUAD 2011/12...

MANAGER
André Villas-Boas. Aged 33

GOALIES
1. Petr Čech. Aged 29

GOALIES
40. Henrique Hilário. Aged 35

GOALIES
22. Ross Turnbull. Aged 26

Do you share a birthday with a Chelsea star? Which is the only month without a
Chelsea birthday? August 24th: Bosingwa ... September 1st: Sturridge ...

DEFENDERS
2. Branislav Ivanovic. Aged 27

DEFENDERS
3. Ashley Cole. Aged 30

DEFENDERS
4. David Luíz. Aged 24

DEFENDERS
19. Paulo Ferreira. Aged 32

DEFENDERS
17. Jose Bosingwa. Aged 28

... September 24th: Romeu ... October 17th: Villas-Boas ... October 21st: Hilário ...

November 13th: Bruma ... December 3rd: Essien ... December 7th: Terry ...

CHELSEA SQUAD 2011/12...

DEFENDERS
33. Alex. Aged 29

DEFENDERS
26. John Terry. Aged 30

MIDFIELDERS
5. Michael Essien. Aged 28

MIDFIELDERS
6. Oriol Romeu. Aged 19

...December 20th: Cole ... January 4th: Turnbull ... January 8th: Mellis ...

January 18th: Ferreira ... February 22nd: Ivanovic ... March 1st: McEachran ...

MIDFIELDERS
15. Florent Malouda. Aged 31

MIDFIELDERS
8. Frank Lampard. Aged 33

MIDFIELDERS
20. Josh McEachran. Aged 18

MIDFIELDERS
7. Ramires. Aged 24

... March 11th: Drogba ... March 14th: Anelka ... March 17th: Miereles ...

March 20th: Torres ... March 24th: Ramires ... April 22nd: Luíz, Mikel ...

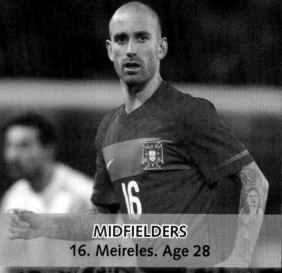

MIDFIELDERS
16. Meireles. Age 28

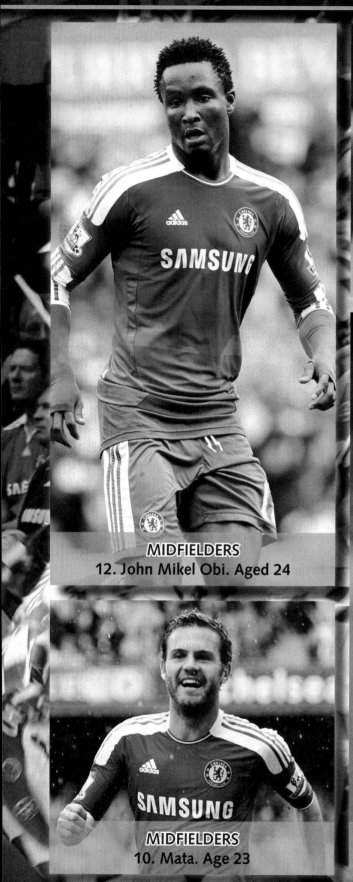

MIDFIELDERS
12. John Mikel Obi. Aged 24

ATTACKERS
9. Fernando Torres. Aged 27

MIDFIELDERS
10. Mata. Age 23

... April 28th: Mata ... May 13th: Lukaku ... May 20th: Čech ... May 13th: Lukaku ...
June 13th: Malouda ... June 17th: Alex ... June 20th: Lampard.

ATTACKERS
21. Salomon Kalou. Aged 26

ATTACKERS
39. Nicolas Anelka. Aged 32

ATTACKERS
11. Didier Drogba. Aged 33

ATTACKERS
23. Daniel Sturridge. Aged 21

ATTACKERS
36. Romelu Lukaku. Aged 18

Did you guess correctly?

The only month without a Chelsea birthday is July.

LONDON 2012 - OLYMPICS FEVER

The biggest sports events in the world, the Olympic Games and Paralympic Games, come to London in 2012. Chelsea Football Club has supported London 2012 since 2004, and everyone is excited about the capital hosting such a huge event.

The Games will be staged at venues all over the south-east of England, and don't worry if you don't have tickets: some of the events are free to view – you just turn up on the day.

Here we offer a few ideas about how to catch some sport live, as well as highlighting some famous Chelsea Olympians.

LONDON 2012

Catch the Olympics for FREE

You do not need a ticket to see some open-air events. People can line the routes of the Olympic race walks, marathons, road cycling and road cycling time-trial races.

The race walks are the easiest to follow as they are made up of many laps of a short circuit in beautiful surroundings of St James's Park and Green Park in the centre of London. They begin and end on The Mall.

The 26-mile marathons also start and finish on The Mall, taking in the Thames embankment before weaving around the ancient streets of the old City of London.

If you live in west London or Surrey the cycling will be easy to see. The cycling road race begins and ends at The Mall in central London. It covers 156 miles (87 miles for women) and runs through Fulham, Putney, Richmond, Kingston, Twickenham, Bushy Park, Weybridge, Woking, Guildford, Dorking, Headley Heath, Leatherhead, and Esher along the way.

The cycling time-trial races take place along a route that starts and finishes at Hampton Court Palace, and runs through Kingston Bridge, Bushy Park, around Bessborough Reservoir, Claremont Landscape Garden and parts of Esher.

OLYMPIC BLUES

RAMIRES

Football bronze medal winner, Beijing 2008

Our current midfielder was a late call-up to Brazil's squad for the Games in 2008 – he replaced Robinho. He made four appearances in China and helped earn his country a bronze medal.

NILS MIDDELBÖE

Football silver medal winner (x2), London 1908 & Stockholm 1912

Nils Middelböe, Chelsea's 'great Dane', won a silver medal at both Olympics he entered. He scored the first ever goal in an Olympics football match against France at London 1908. His brothers Einar and Kristian also represented Denmark. Nils was also his country's record-holder at triple jump and 800 metres running.

SALOMON KALOU

Football, Beijing 2008

Faced a young Argentina side featuring Lionel Messi and it was his solitary goal that took 'the Elephants' into the quarter-finals, where they lost to Nigeria.

DID YOU KNOW?

Chelsea's shirt sponsor, Samsung, is one of the sponsors of the Olympics, including the Olympic Torch Relay as it makes its way around the UK.

BENJAMIN HOWARD BAKER

High jump, standing high jump, triple jump, Stockholm 1912 & Antwerp 1920

One of the most eccentric goalkeepers in Chelsea's history, Ben arrived as a former UK record-holder at the high jump. He had competed in athletics events at Stamford Bridge before playing football there in the 1920s. He was renowned for playing basketball with the ball around his area, and is the only keeper to have scored a goal in an official match for Chelsea. An all-round athlete, the best he finished for GB was sixth in the high jump in 1920.

CELESTINE BABAYARO

Football gold medal winner (1996), Atlanta 1996 & Sydney 2000

Chelsea paid a club record £2.25m for a teenager when signing him from Anderlecht in 1997. Celestine (middle name Hyacinth) had played left-back for Nigeria the year before and won the gold medal, and had scored in the final against Argentina. He captained the Nigerians in Australia four years later, without repeating the previous success.

VIVIAN 'JACK' WOODWARD (right)

Football gold medal winner (x2), London 1908 & Stockholm 1912

Gentleman centre-forward Jack Woodward was one of the most popular Chelsea players of his day. He was also Great Britain's hero, skippering the national football team to the gold medal twice in 1908 and 1912. On both occasions the opponents in the final were Denmark, and his future Stamford Bridge teammate, Nils Middelböe.

DID YOU KNOW?

London 2012 organiser Lord Coe is a lifelong Chelsea fan.

JOHN 'JACK' BUDD

Water Polo, Paris 1924 & Amsterdam 1928

Jack Budd was 6'7", could swim 100 yards in 63 seconds and represented Great Britain in two Olympics at water polo. He was part of the GB team that finished fourth at the 1928 Games. A few years later, in 1931, Budd became a director of Chelsea FC board and was afterwards appointed vice-chairman until his death in 1952.

THE 500 CLUB

In all our history just five players have made 500 or more appearances for Chelsea. Two new people joined this exclusive club last season: Frank Lampard and John Terry.

Here we profile each member of the club and find out why they were so special.

Ron Harris

795

Appearances: 795

Debut: February 1962 v Sheffield Wednesday (League Division One)

Career highlights: FA Cup 1970, Uefa Cup-Winners' Cup 1971, League Cup 1965

Fact: As captain, **'Chopper'** Harris once knocked Italy's mighty AC Milan out of the Fairs Cup – by winning the toss of a coin.

Peter Bonetti

729

APPEARANCES: 729

DEBUT: April 1960 v Manchester City (League Division One)

CAREER HIGHLIGHTS: FA Cup 1970, Uefa Cup-Winners' Cup 1971, League Cup 1965. Chelsea Player of the Year 1967

FACT: **'The Cat'** was a member of England's World Cup squad in 1966 – but only received his winners' medal from FIFA in 2009!

John Hollins

592

APPEARANCES: 592

DEBUT: September 1963 v Swindon Town (League Cup)

CAREER HIGHLIGHTS: FA Cup 1970, Uefa Cup-Winners' Cup 1971, League Cup 1965. Chelsea Player of the Year 1970, 1971

FACT: 'Holly' had two playing spells at Stamford Bridge – and went on to become manager of the Blues in the 1980s

Frank Lampard

509

APPEARANCES: 509

DEBUT: August 2001 v Newcastle (Premier League)

CAREER HIGHLIGHTS: Premier League 2005, 2006, 2010, FA Cup 2007, 2009, 2010, League Cup 2005, 2007. Chelsea Player of the Year 2004, 2005, 2009

FACT: 'Lamps' is the only member of the '500 Club' who was not a former Chelsea youth team player

John Terry

501

APPEARANCES: 501

DEBUT: October 1998 v Aston Villa (League Cup)

CAREER HIGHLIGHTS: Premier League 2005, 2006, 2010, FA Cup 2000, 2007, 2009, 2010, League Cup 2005, 2007. Chelsea Player of the Year 2001, 2006

FACT: The only team other than Chelsea that JT has played for is Nottingham Forest – during a loan spell in 1999/2000

All statistics correct up to the end of 2010/11 season

SPOT THE REAL BALL

We've added an extra 7 footballs to this photograph taken during a match. Can you work out which is the real ball?

Answer on Page 61

Brazilliance!
Chelsea's Samba Boys

Chelsea have always welcomed the best overseas talent, right from our earliest days. And on Boxing Day 1999 at Southampton we became the first club to field a team with no Englishmen in it, winning 2-1 with both goals coming from a Norwegian: Tore-Andre Flo. Chelsea had hired top players from everywhere: Australia, Europe and Africa. Yet South America, which has always produced so many superstar footballers, was different.

Alex hits an unstoppable free kick against Birmingham City

It's true that a few years earlier we had signed the influential and hugely popular Uruguayan Gustavo Poyet, and in that December of 1999 our first Brazilian had arrived: Emerson Thome.

Emerson was a fast, strong, no-nonsense, English-style defender. He was not the skilful, tricky, flair player we instantly think of when Brazil is mentioned, such as Pele, Kaká or Ronaldinho.

More than seven years later, the next to arrive was another defender, Alex. Chelsea brought him over from PSV Eindhoven in 2007. He was another tall, powerful central defender, but he introduced the Brazilian skill of firing swirling, long-distant free kicks to Stamford Bridge and is loved by fans.

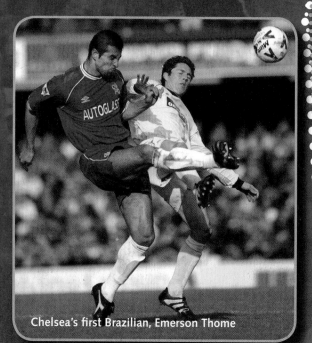
Chelsea's first Brazilian, Emerson Thome

DID YOU KNOW?
Chelsea's first ever match under floodlights was in Rio de Janeiro, Brazil, in 1929.

At the same time, Juliano Belletti arrived. The man from Cascavel was a full-back who liked to attack and shoot.

His eye for the net brought him five goals, including one scorcher against Spurs that was voted Goal of the Season 2007/8.

Juliano Belletti, scoring against Middlesbrough

Deco showing his skill

The Brazilian-born Portugal international Deco arrived from Barcelona in 2008. Here, at last, was a really skilful attacking midfielder.

But Deco was nearly 31 when he arrived at Stamford Bridge, and injuries meant he did not play much. Even when Chelsea had the Brazilian manager, Luis Felipe Scolari, things did not work out for Deco.

DID YOU KNOW? ❓
Chelsea played a friendly against top Brazilian club Santos, including the great Pele, in Jamaica on 2 February 1971.

Midfield trickery from Ramires.

So you could say that Brazilian samba football was in short supply at the Bridge – until the arrival last season of a further two South American stars: Ramires and David Luiz.

Ramires, signed from Benfica, Portugal, in the summer of 2010 is a fantastically hard-working midfielder who has been called the 'blue Kenyan' because he has the endurance of a long-distance runner.

His career at Chelsea really took off when he skipped through Man City's defence to score the winner against them. That was proper Brazilian flair.

Just before then, at the end of January 2011, another samba star arrived: David Luiz Moreira Marinho.

David is another centre-back, but very different from the others. He has the combination of skill, amazing technique and imagination that has people jumping out of their seats. Just like when he scored against Manchester United in only his third Chelsea appearance.

David has had the biggest impact of all Chelsea's Brazilians. He was quickly admired even by opposition supporters and voted Premier League Player of the Month.

David Luiz,
after scoring against
Man City

DOING THE RIGHT THING

It's not all about glory and winning. Chelsea Football Club aims to give a lot back to the community at home and abroad. The club supports two main charities. Our national charity partner is Help A Capital Child, run by 95.8 Capital FM. Globally, we work with Right To Play.

Chelsea has helped raise vital funds since linking up with Help A Capital Child to improve the lives of young Londoners.

'One in three children in London live below the poverty line,' says Capital FM's breakfast show presenter – and massive Blues fan – Johnny Vaughan. 'It's easy to think that poverty is an issue for someone else, that it happens overseas in the developing world, but there are over half a million young people right here in London who are living in poverty.

'You're never more than a mile from a project funded by the charity. Charity begins at home. London is the home of Chelsea FC - these are our children!'

RIGHT TO PLAY

Right To Play uses sport projects to enhance the lives of young people around the world.

Francis Ebo Turkson, a Right To Play coordinator in Ghana, has seen the big positive effect the projects have on children. 'Naturally, physical activity gets them moving,' he said, 'and it helps them concentrate when they go back into the classroom but it also develops their mind, body and soul. 'These values help them in the classroom and within their surrounding community, things such as compassion, team work and a lot of other things that will help them to do well in their communities. 'The things these children learn through play will stay with them forever.'

THE CHELSEA FOUNDATION

The Chelsea Foundation uses the power of football to help change our communities. Through the use of sport we help tackle crime, social exclusion and anti-social behaviour while promoting health, education and stronger safer communities.

Every year we work with over one million predominantly young people providing coaching, workshops and positive diversions as well as offering specialist numeracy, literacy and IT programmes for both pupils and adults.
Our soccer schools, which take place during the school holidays, provide professional coaching and allow children to showcase their talents at the Cobham training ground. On top of that our anti-discrimination work is helping tackle prejudice both at Stamford Bridge and our wider community.

To find out more about the work of the Foundation please visit our website at www.chelseafc.com/foundation

Essien's 'Reading Goals' initiative, Ghana

CAREFREE:
Wherever You May Be

Chelsea's motto for the pre-season tour of Asia in 2011 was 'Here to play, here to stay' and the club has been winning millions of lifelong supporters all around the world in recent years.

Most of them will never be lucky enough to visit Stamford Bridge, but they will support us from afar and often with as much fanaticism as someone born on the King's Road, Chelsea.

ASIA:

Chelsea were mobbed everywhere they went in Asia this summer. At the airport in the Malaysian capital city, Kuala Lumpur, it was as if Justin Bieber had arrived when Frank Lampard walked past the security barriers.

The Blues are helping to promote football in the region by building blue football pitches for local youngsters.

An incredible 84,980 noisy fans were in the sold out National Stadium, Bukit Jalil, to see Chelsea beat a Malaysia XI 1-0 in July 2011.

AMERICA:

Hollywood actress Charlize Theron, a big Chelsea fan, was one of 81,224 faces in the crowd at the Rose Bowl stadium, Pasadena, LA, in July 2009. The Blues were playing Internazionale of Milan, Italy, as part of a tour of the United States.

The team played three more matches, and the average attendance at all of them was 68,736 – a record for a visiting soccer team playing four games in the USA.

From coast to coast across America, Chelsea are one of the most popular teams in football – soccer as they call it there.

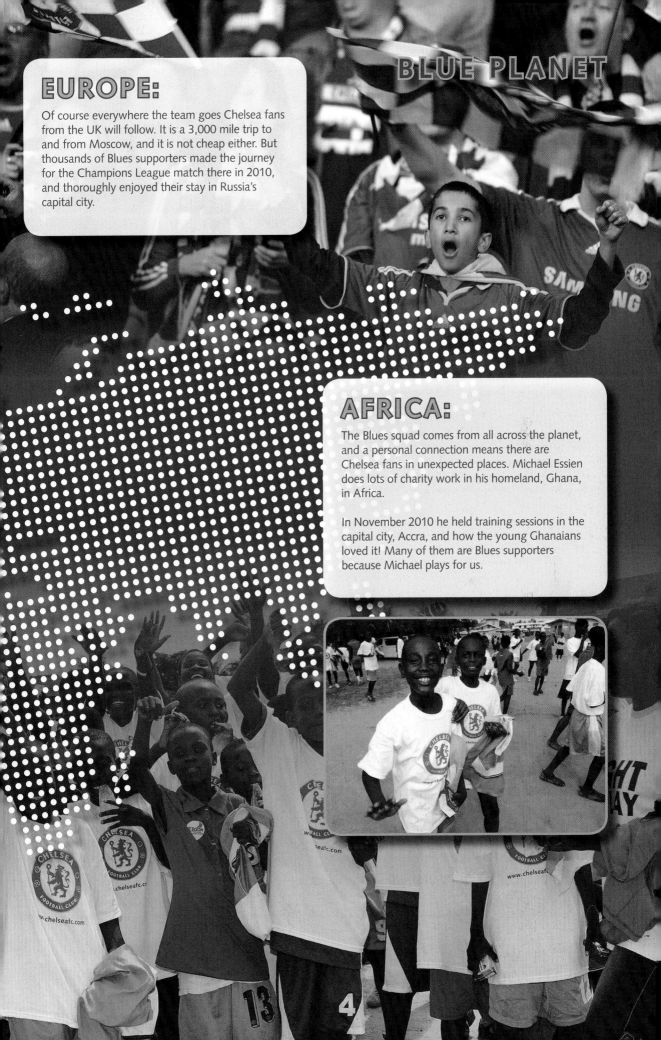

EUROPE:

Of course everywhere the team goes Chelsea fans from the UK will follow. It is a 3,000 mile trip to and from Moscow, and it is not cheap either. But thousands of Blues supporters made the journey for the Champions League match there in 2010, and thoroughly enjoyed their stay in Russia's capital city.

AFRICA:

The Blues squad comes from all across the planet, and a personal connection means there are Chelsea fans in unexpected places. Michael Essien does lots of charity work in his homeland, Ghana, in Africa.

In November 2010 he held training sessions in the capital city, Accra, and how the young Ghanaians loved it! Many of them are Blues supporters because Michael plays for us.

YOUNG, GIFTED ...
AND BLUE

How many of you reading this dream of putting on the famous royal blue and running out of the tunnel at Stamford Bridge?

Each year hundreds of children attend training sessions organised by the club, and some boys are selected to train regularly at Cobham.

Eventually, with enough natural talent and hard work, they may find themselves one of the lucky lads attending the Chelsea Academy.

Even then most youngsters don't make it into the Reserves team – let alone a higher level.

But some gifted teenagers are making it into the first team alongside JT and Drog. Here we highlight just a few of the youngsters to look out for this season.

'HOPEFULLY I WILL SPEND MY CAREER AT CHELSEA. I HAVE WANTED TO DO THAT SINCE I WAS A KID, SINCE I JOINED WHEN I WAS EIGHT YEARS OLD. HOPEFULLY I WILL PLAY MORE GAMES AND KEEP IMPROVING'

JOSH MCEACHRAN

JOSH MCEACHRAN
Born Mar 1993. Silkily-skilled attacking midfielder capable of breathtaking dribbles and passing. England Under-21 international. Signed a new five-year contract in July.

RYAN BERTRAND

Born Aug 1989. Fast, technical and attacking left-back who produces dangerous crosses. England Under-21 international. Signed a contract in the summer that will keep him at the Bridge till 2015.

"I CAN SEE THE MANAGER IS YOUNG AND HUNGRY AND WANTS TO TAKE THE CLUB FORWARD SO I WANT TO BE PART OF THAT"

RYAN BERTRAND

NATHANIEL CHALOBAH

Born Dec 1994. Skilful, focused central defender or midfielder, a great leader for his age. England Under-17s skipper who has played for the first team in pre-season matches.

BILLY CLIFFORD

Born Oct 1992. Exciting right-back or midfielder renowned for his powerful attacking runs. An unused sub for the Champions League game in Moscow last season.

YOUNG, GIFTED ...
AND BLUE

JAMAL BLACKMAN
Born Oct 1993. Agile, hard-working 6'5" goalkeeper with a very good attitude. England Under-17 international.

Patrick Van Aanholt
Born Aug 1990. He scored a first Chelsea goal against Newcastle in the Carling Cup. He signed a new four-year contract with Chelsea in May 2011.

WORDSEARCH

Use your detective skills to find the 20 player names in the grid below.
They go up, down, backwards or diagonally. See if you can spot them all.

A	K	D	L	K	T	W	T	B	D	R	O	G	B	A	M
M	R	N	R	T	L	X	L	K	P	X	L	D	R	E	K
R	L	I	D	A	H	U	L	Z	H	J	D	D	U	S	Y
N	L	S	E	G	P	Q	I	M	C	Y	X	O	C	S	A
A	R	E	T	R	H	M	A	Z	E	T	L	I	L	I	C
R	B	R	G	G	R	L	A	D	C	A	V	T	L	E	S
H	Z	R	F	K	O	E	N	L	K	O	W	T	U	N	O
C	V	O	R	U	D	Z	F	Y	N	T	C	M	B	K	I
A	M	T	D	L	A	M	N	A	D	F	J	X	N	C	B
E	I	A	M	T	Q	R	V	M	L	Y	Z	D	R	K	X
C	K	Y	A	X	O	I	R	L	L	U	Z	K	U	X	C
M	E	M	K	M	B	N	W	Z	H	P	K	Y	T	X	H
W	L	K	E	A	W	G	N	I	S	O	B	A	M	C	Q
M	M	U	C	O	L	E	K	T	E	R	R	Y	K	P	B
N	Z	L	M	S	E	R	I	M	A	R	B	L	W	U	Z
R	T	K	N	R	O	C	H	A	K	T	J	B	R	D	R

BOSINGWA	ESSIEN	LAMPARD	MATA	ROMEU
CECH	FERREIRA	LUIZ	MCEACHRAN	TERRY
COLE	IVANOVIC	LUKAKU	MIKEL	TORRES
DROGBA	KALOU	MALOUDA	RAMIRES	TURNBULL

Answer on Page 61

SPOT THE DIFFERENCE

Can you spot the 8 differences between the pictures below?

Answer on Page 61

CHELSEA MUSEUM & STADIUM TOURS

BRAND NEW MUSEUM

THE ULTIMATE FOOTBALL EXPERIENCE

FOR BOOKINGS VISIT CHELSEAFC.COM/TOURS
OR CALL 0871 984 1955

Tours do not run on home match days or the day prior to champion's league home matches. Tours are subject to availability, change and cancellation at short notice

Where's Stamford?

Can you spot Stamford in the picture below?

Chelsea Awards Evening 2011

On 19 May 2011, during a glitzy evening at Stamford Bridge, the bravest and the best of Chelsea's season were handed awards for their work. Here is the low-down on who won what.

YOUNG PLAYER OF THE YEAR

Chelsea's Young Player of the Year was named as Josh McEachran. When he came on for his debut away to MSK Žilina he was the first player to appear in the Champions League who was born after its formation from the old European Cup in 1992.

THE HOST

Awards Evening host Mark Austin (from ITV news) is a Chelsea season ticket-holder. He interviewed the winners and those who announced them, including former Chelsea manager Tommy Docherty.

GOAL OF THE SEASON

There were several good contenders, but Ramires' clever run and shot against Manchester City won Goal of the Season. The Brazil midfielder was delighted.

PLAYERS' PLAYER OF THE YEAR

This is an award voted for by the players themselves. This season the winner was Ashley Cole who, alongside Petr Cech, was Chelsea's only ever-present player in the Premier League.

PLAYER OF THE YEAR

Petr Cech was the runaway winner of the evening's biggest award. The big Czech was back to his very best, making countless vital saves, including a penalty against Fulham. He's the fourth goalie to win the trophy since Peter Bonetti won the first way back in 1967.

SPECIAL RECOGNITION AWARD

This award is given to those whose Chelsea connections go back a long way. This year former defensive partner John Dempsey handed it over to Ron Harris. Ron skippered the Blues to victory in the 1970 FA Cup and 1971 Uefa Cup-Winners' Cup and made a record 795 appearances for the Blues.

Treasures of the Chelsea Museum

The Zoo has its penguins, the Tower has its Crown Jewels, but for Chelsea supporters no London attraction is greater than the new Chelsea Museum.

Massively expanded, with loads more fun and interactive parts, it is a must for Blues fans of all ages, with something for followers old and new. Featured over the next few pages are just some of the must-see exhibits.

The Trophies...

Only Man United have won more silverware in the Premier League era, so we have plenty of bling on show these days. You can take a good look at lots of trophies: the three Premier League ones, the 1955 Football League Championship, FA Cups, Uefa Cup-Winners' Cups and League Cups. Oh, and take a look at the shirts the players wore in some of the games. One of them is almost 50 years old.

The Famous Shirts...

Lots of Chelsea players past and present have donated shirts they have worn in famous matches to the museum. Plenty of them are on display through a brilliant machine that allows you to select and see any shirt of your choice, with information about who wore it and when.

The Surprising Colour...

Bet you didn't know that Chelsea's first kit was not the colour we all know now, but a much lighter greeny-blue. That is one of several surprises – even for diehard supporters – to be found at the museum. The 1905 shirts were based on the horseracing colours of our first club president, Lord Cadogan. The current Earl Cadogan has donated a set of racing silks so that you can imagine what the first Chelsea players would have worn.

A 100-Year-Old Football...

Ever wondered what a really old football looks like? Wonder no more. On display at the museum is the very ball carried by Chelsea captain Nils Middelböe for the game against Derby County in November 1913. He played in midfield and was named man of the match afterwards.

He was presented with the ball afterwards as a memento, and his descendants in Denmark returned it to Chelsea in 2011. It still has some of the original air pumped into it.

MONEY-SAVING TIP:

it's cheaper to book your visit in advance online, and you can do just that here:
www.chelseafc.com/museum

Agility Of A Cat?

The challenge is: 'Do you have reactions like The Cat?' Who is The Cat? That's Peter Bonetti, the longest-serving goalkeeper in our history, and one of the most popular Chelsea players of the 1960s and 1970s. He was not very tall but amazingly agile and renowned for springing to make incredible saves.

In this brilliant game, you have to hit the buttons as quickly as you can as soon as they light up. Your score appears at the end. Believe us, it's very hard! (Or maybe we're just slow!).

Chelsea In The Trenches

During World War I Chelsea donated 50 footballs to soldiers in the trenches – one of them may have been used in the famous Christmas Truce football matches with the Germans in No-Man's-Land.

The museum also tells the tragic story about former goalie 'Pom-Pom' Whiting, who was in the Footballers' Battalion and died in battle before he could even see his newly-born son.

CHELSEA'S GREATEST GOALIES

In May 2011 Petr Cech became the fifth goalkeeper to win the coveted Player of the Year award. He was the best player of the 2010/11 season, but is he Chelsea's best ever man between the sticks?

CHELSEA'S GREATEST GOALIES

PETR CECH (DEBUT 2004)
Holds the Premier League record for requiring the fewest matches to reach 100 clean sheets: 180.

APPEARANCES: 313

CLEAN SHEETS: 159

CONSISTENCY: 9

AGILITY: 9

KEY SKILLS: Tall, dominant and almost certainly the best shot-stopper in the business today.

CHELSEA'S GREATEST GOALIES

VIC WOODLEY (1931)
Also England's no.1 in the 1930s, Vic kept Chelsea's Scotland keeper, Johnny Jackson, out of the side.

APPEARANCES: 272

CLEAN SHEETS: 60

CONSISTENCY: 8

AGILITY: 8

KEY SKILLS: Unflappable in the days when strikers were allowed to charge into keepers.

CHELSEA'S GREATEST GOALIES

BILL ROBERTSON (1951)
Actually fainted before making his nerve-wracking debut, but recovered to keep Chelsea in the top flight.

APPEARANCES: 213

CLEAN SHEETS: 38

CONSISTENCY: 6

AGILITY: 7

KEY SKILLS: His big, safe hands and anticipation of danger were second to none.

STAR KEEPER

CHELSEA'S GREATEST GOALIES

SAM MILLINGTON (1926)
Renowned for wearing a flat cap whenever he played.

APPEARANCES: 255

CLEAN SHEETS: 78

CONSISTENCY: 8

AGILITY: 7

KEY SKILLS: One of the best at jumping and punching the ball away from the danger area.

CHELSEA'S GREATEST GOALIES

BEN HOWARD BAKER (1921)
The only Chelsea goalie ever to have scored a goal in a game: from the penalty spot.

APPEARANCES: 255

CLEAN SHEETS: 78

CONSISTENCY: 6

AGILITY: 9

KEY SKILLS: Acrobatics; he was also a champion high jumper in athletics.

CHELSEA'S GREATEST GOALIES

EDDIE NIEDZWIECKI (1983)
Brilliant Wales international who was at his peak when injury ended his career.

APPEARANCES: 169

CLEAN SHEETS: 55

CONSISTENCY: 8

AGILITY: 8

KEY SKILLS: Complete all-rounder who was extremely reliable.

CHELSEA'S GREATEST GOAL

PETER BONETTI (1960)
Chelsea's longest-serving goalkeeper, the best over three decades.

APPEARANCES: 729

CLEAN SHEETS: 208

CONSISTENCY: 8

AGILITY: 9

KEY SKILLS: Overcoming lack of height with amazing leap and flexibility.

CHELSEA'S GREATEST GOALIES

ED DE GOEY (1997)
Set a club record in 1999/2000 by making 59 appearances and keeping 27 clean sheets in that season.

APPEARANCES: 179

CLEAN SHEETS: 71

CONSISTENCY: 8

AGILITY: 6

KEY SKILLS: Excellent focus and positioning.

QUIZ ANSWERS:

Spot the Real Ball, Page 28

Wordsearch, Page 45

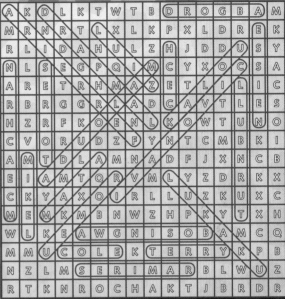

Spot the Difference, Page 48

G⚽AL RUSH!

The 2010/11 season brought another crop of great strikes, and we have picked out ten of the best. Which one was your favourite?

Didier Drogba v Arsenal October 2010
Ramires pass split defence, Ash cuts the ball back, Drogba brilliant back-heel.

GOAL OF THE SEASON
RAMIRES V MANCHESTER CITY MARCH 2011
The Brazilian midfielder weaves his way through three City defenders before smashing the ball past Joe Hart.

Alex v Arsenal October 2010
Thumping, swerving free kick from the Brazilian, 30 yards out. Gunners' keeper Fabianski was beaten all ends up.

Yury Zhirkov v Spartak Moscow October 2010
A Moscow defender heads out feebly, and the Russian midfielder catches the ball sweetly in his instep, looping the ball over the stranded goalie.